How To Draw Cute Heroes

HOW TO DRAW CUTE HEROES

 Dawn MacDonald

Search Press

Published in 2020 by
Search Press Ltd
Wellwood
North Farm Rd
Tunbridge Wells
Kent TN2 3DR

A QUARTO BOOK

ISBN-13: 978-1-78221-924-8

QUAR.335795

Conceived, designed and produced by Quarto Publishing plc.
6 Blundell Street, London N7 9BH

Senior Commissioning Editor: Eszter Karpati
Editor: Katie Hardwicke
Art Director: Gemma Wilson
Deputy Art Director: Martina Calvio
Designer: Clare Barber
Illustrator: Dawn MacDonald
Publisher: Samantha Warrington

Printed in China

10 9 8 7 6 5 4 3 2 1

CONTENTS

INTRODUCTION

Hello! My name is Dawn MacDonald, and I've been an avid artist since the tender age of six years old, when I discovered pencils and paper. The first things I loved to draw were cartoons and dragons, and as the years progressed, I developed a thirst for drawing anything and everything.

I was thrilled to be given the opportunity in this book to draw some of the most prominent people in history, from the worlds of art and music – subjects that have inspired and motivated me – to science and sport, in a cute and easy style that every young artist can follow to advance their own drawing skills.

Each character is drawn in stages, starting with basic guides that plot the main shapes of the pose. Sketch these lightly, as you will draw your final artwork on top. Follow each step and the drawing will come together using outlines that can be coloured when you're finished.

Work through the book to discover pivotal figures of art, activism, music, science, literature and sports – people from the past and those making a difference now. Practise makes perfect, so follow the tutorials to progress your art – take inspiration from the heroes and heroines to get drawing and keep practicing!

ART MATERIALS

THERE ARE SO MANY DIFFERENT TOOLS YOU CAN USE TO DRAW AND COLOUR CUTE HEROES. THESE ARE SOME OF THE MATERIALS THAT I LOVE THE MOST.

PAPER

You don't need a specific kind of paper; any drawing surface is fine, but a gridded paper will help you to plot the guides. Use a sketchbook or notebook if you want to keep all your drawings together. If you like to paint use a thicker paper, as it won't wrinkle as much.

PENS

These are my favourite tool! Pens are great when you want a thin stroke or a precise line. They are perfect for facial expressions and details. Try technical drawing pens to get a perfect line for borders and straight edges.

MARKERS

These have wide nibs that leave thicker, permanent marks. Test them first as you can't erase the lines you make. Some art markers are light and create beautiful thick, paint-like strokes, perfect for colouring in!

CRAYONS

If you're going to be doing a lot of colouring, crayons can be fun. You can create thin strokes by lightly pressing or press harder for rich colours and thicker lines.

PENCILS

Graphite pencil leads are graded hard (H or #3) or soft (B for black or #1). Some artists prefer the H pencil because it makes a very slight, grey line, which is perfect for light guidelines, but the lead can scratch the paper if you press too hard.

Mechanical pencils are refillable and designed to take a variety of leads. The advantage of a mechanical pencil is that it is sharp all the time, so the lead widths give you the choice of how delicate you want the pencil point to be and how thick or thin the line.

Coloured pencils are ideal for sketching and creating fun accessories and outfits. Choose between traditional wooden pencils or mechanical pencils.

WATERCOLOURS

Available in a palette or a tube in a vast range of colours, high-quality artists' watercolours are usually worth the extra cost. A pan of watercolours is easily portable, or use tube colours for creating washes.

Whether you use paints, pencils, pens or crayons, you need to think about what is most comfortable for you. Experiment with different colours, textures and line widths to see your cute heroes really come to life!

BRUSHES

You might prefer to paint your cute heroes, rather than draw them, or you could draw first, then paint. You will need two types of brushes: a thin brush for drawing and one or more round brushes for applying colour. It can be a bit awkward to draw with a brush, as you have less control than with a pen.

LEADERS AND ACTIVISTS

MARLEY DIAS

MAHATMA GANDHI

LET'S START DRAWING MAHATMA GANDHI – A REVOLUTIONARY LAWYER WHO LED THE INDIAN CAMPAIGN FOR INDEPENDENCE FROM BRITISH COLONIAL RULE. HE WAS A GREAT POLITICIAN WHO PRACTICED NON-VIOLENCE AND BECAME KNOWN AS THE FATHER OF THE NATION, INSPIRING MILLIONS OF PEOPLE!

Start by drawing the basic guides that form Gandhi's body.

1

Draw his head shape and add his ears.

2

Next, draw his glasses and the frames.

3

4

Now draw his
eyes, facial
features and
hairline.

5

Sketch his
upper body
and clothes.

6

Now draw his
lower body and
sandalled feet.

Here's how your
artwork should look
once you've drawn
everything. Great
work!

HARRIET TUBMAN

BORN INTO SLAVERY IN THE 1820s, HARRIET TUBMAN ESCAPED AND BECAME AN AMERICAN ABOLITIONIST AND POLITICAL ACTIVIST. SHE HELPED RESCUE HUNDREDS OF ENSLAVED PEOPLE USING A NETWORK OF SAFE HOUSES, KNOWN AS THE UNDERGROUND RAILROAD. LET'S PAY TRIBUTE TO HER COURAGE AND DRAW HER!

Start by drawing the guidelines for her face and body.

1

Next, add her facial features.

2

Add her hair and face shape.

3

Now draw the
upper body and
her clasped
hands.

4

Once that's
done, work on
Harriet's skirt.

5

Lastly, fill in the
final touches,
like her shoes
and the detailing
on her clothes.

6

Be proud of your
finished piece and
share your drawing!

MALALA YOUSAFZAI

LET'S DRAW MALALA, AN ACTIVIST FOR FEMALE EDUCATION AND THE YOUNGEST NOBEL PRIZE LAUREATE. HAVING SURVIVED AN ATTACK AFTER CONTINUOUSLY SPEAKING OUT ON BEHALF OF GIRLS SEEKING AN EDUCATION, SHE HAS BECOME AN INSPIRING SYMBOL FOR FIGHTING FOR ONE'S BELIEFS.

Start with Malala's guidelines.

1

Then, draw a larger circle outside the guides for her headscarf.

2

Next, draw a smaller circle inside the bigger one.

3

Now, draw her hair and facial features.

Time to draw the rest of her hijab and her hands.

Finally, draw the lower part of her body.

Now you can add some colours and patterns! Great job!

GRETA THUNBERG

GRETA THUNBERG WAS ONLY FIFTEEN WHEN SHE STARTED 'SCHOOL STRIKE FOR CLIMATE' IN SWEDEN. HER CAUSE WAS SOON EMBRACED BY MILLIONS ALL OVER THE WORLD AND CALLS FOR POLITICAL LEADERS TO DO MORE TO PREVENT CLIMATE CHANGE. LET'S DRAW GRETA!

Begin by drawing the basic guides for Greta's pose.

1

Next, add her face shape, hair and mouth.

2

Fill in her eyes, eyebrows and her plaits.

3

Now add a
beanie hat
under her hood.

4

Sketch in her
hood and then
her arms.

5

Finish by
drawing the rest
of her raincoat,
legs and shoes.

6

Compare your
drawing – it should
look like this!
Excellent work,
keep it up!

MARTIN LUTHER KING JR.

IN HIS FAMOUS 'I HAVE A DREAM' SPEECH, MARTIN LUTHER KING JR. CALLED FOR AN END TO RACIAL DISCRIMINATION. LET'S RECREATE THIS INSPIRING PASTOR AND PASSIONATE LEADER OF THE CIVIL RIGHTS MOVEMENT, CHIBI STYLE!

Start with sketching the primary guides.

1

Draw the head shape for Martin.

2

Now sketch his facial features, hairline and ears.

3

Move on to sketching the torso and arms.

4

Draw the rest of his suit, shirt and tie.

5

6

Then, draw his trousers and shoes.

7

Lastly, sketch a microphone and stand for him to speak into.

Your final drawing should resemble this. How easy was that?

ABRAHAM LINCOLN

STATESMAN AND HERO, 'HONEST ABE', WAS THE 16TH PRESIDENT OF THE UNITED STATES. HE IS REMEMBERED FOR HIS MANY ACHIEVEMENTS, INCLUDING ABOLISHING SLAVERY, MODERNIZING THE US ECONOMY AND LEADING THE NATION THROUGH THE AMERICAN CIVIL WAR.

Begin by drawing the guidelines for Abe.

1

Next, draw the beginnings of his face.

2

Then, sketch in his facial features and the first stages of hair.

3

4

Go ahead and sketch his hat!

5

Then, draw the left side of his body.

6

Continue to draw the right side of his body.

7

Lastly, sketch his legs and shoes.

Your final sketch should resemble this. Very smart!

BARACK OBAMA

OBAMA WAS THE 44TH PRESIDENT OF THE UNITED STATES AND THE FIRST AFRICAN-AMERICAN PRESIDENT IN US HISTORY. HE WAS AN INSPIRATION FOR MANY PEOPLE – ESPECIALLY AMERICANS FROM DIFFERENT MINORITY ETHNIC GROUPS. LET'S PAY TRIBUTE TO THIS NOBEL PEACE PRIZE WINNER!

Begin by drawing the primary guidelines for Obama.

1

Draw his face shape and ears, leaving a gap on the right ear for his flag overlay.

2

Next, draw his eyes, eyebrows and mouth.

3

Now draw his hairline.

Next, add his raised right arm and a flag in his hand.

4

5

Sketch his left arm and then the rest of his body.

6

7

Lastly, finish drawing Obama's legs and shoes.

Take a moment to admire your drawing – you're becoming a pro!

JAZZ JENNINGS

HAVE SOME COLOURS READY FOR WHEN YOU'VE FINISHED DRAWING YOUTUBE STAR AND LGBT ACTIVIST, JAZZ JENNINGS. ONE OF THE YOUNGEST PUBLICLY KNOWN PEOPLE TO BE IDENTIFIED AS TRANSGENDER, HER BRAVERY IS AN INSPIRATION FOR PEOPLE OF ANY AGE.

Begin drawing the guidelines for Jazz's body.

1

Then, draw her face and hairline.

2

Take your time to draw her long, pretty hair.

3

Finish her hair by drawing the flower headband.

4

Now it's time to draw her eyes and mouth.

5

Then, sketch her upper body with her interlocking hands.

6

7

Lastly, draw the rest of the upper and lower parts of her dress.

You've finished drawing Jazz! Time to add lots of colour!

MANAL AL-SHARIF

FAMOUS FOR HER CAMPAIGN TO GIVE WOMEN THE RIGHT TO DRIVE IN SAUDI ARABIA, ACTIVIST AND COLUMNIST MANAL AL-SHARIF IS LIVING PROOF THAT ONE VOICE CAN MAKE A DIFFERENCE IN THE WORLD! READY TO DRAW HER?

Start by sketching her basic body guides.

1

Now draw her face shape and the edge of her headscarf.

2

Next, draw Manal's facial features – her mouth and eyes.

3

Now draw her headscarf, or hijab, that drapes below her neck.

Start to draw her upper body, arms and hands – don't forget the microphone.

Work on drawing her lower body next and the microphone cord.

Finish by filling in the pattern for her headscarf.

All finished! Turn the page to learn about another person who has impacted our world.

MARLEY DIAS

LET'S PUT PEN TO PAPER FOR SOCIAL ACTIVIST MARLEY! HER CAMPAIGN #1000BLACKGIRLBOOKS, DREW ATTENTION TO THE LACK OF DIVERSITY IN CHILDREN'S BOOKS. SHE STARTED HER MOVEMENT IN 2015, WHEN SHE WAS ONLY TWELVE YEARS OLD.

Start with the simple guidelines to build her body.

1

2

Then, draw Marley's head shape followed by her pigtails.

Sketch her eyes and then the glasses that frame them.

3

Now work on drawing her arms and the book she is holding.

4

Let's sketch her lower body and shoes!

5

6

Add shoelaces, and use thin lines to draw the pinstripes on her outfit - or leave it plain if you prefer.

Nicely done! Keep reading and drawing.

STEPHEN HAWKING

ALBERT EINSTEIN

MARIE CURIE

THOMAS EDISON

KATHERINE JOHNSON

ADA LOVELACE

NIKOLA TESLA

STEVE JOBS

ISAAC NEWTON

SACAGAWEA

AMELIA EARHART

THINKERS AND EXPLORERS

MAE JEMISON

NEIL ARMSTRONG

STEPHEN HAWKING

HERE'S A CHANCE TO DRAW THE BRILLIANT ENGLISH THEORETICAL PHYSICIST, COSMOLOGIST AND AUTHOR STEPHEN HAWKING. DESPITE BEING DIAGNOSED WITH THE INCURABLE ILLNESS MND AT AGE 21, HAWKING LIVED FOR ANOTHER 55 YEARS, AND WAS A HUGE SUCCESS – ATTRACTING HUGE CROWDS OF PEOPLE TO HIS LECTURES AND SELLING MILLIONS OF BOOKS.

Begin with the basic guidelines.

1

Then, draw his face shape and ears.

2

Next, sketch his hair and hairline.

3

Then, fill in the facial features and his glasses frames.

4

5

Now sketch his arms.

6

Draw his wheelchair next.

7

Next, sketch his legs and shoes.

8

Then, draw the rest of his wheelchair.

Show off your final line art and think about adding some colour!

ALBERT EINSTEIN

NOW, HERE'S HOW TO DRAW ALBERT EINSTEIN. HE WAS A THEORETICAL PHYSICIST AND ONE OF THE GREATEST SCIENTIFIC MINDS OF ALL TIME. HE IS MOST WELL-KNOWN FOR DEVELOPING THE THEORY OF RELATIVITY AND THE EQUATION E=MC².

Begin by drawing the guides for Einstein.

1

Then, draw the simple face shape.

2

Now work on the hair shape for Einstein.

3

4 Next, draw his eyes and other facial features.

5 Now draw his body. Begin with the outer shape.

Finish with his feet, clothes and the hand holding his pointer.

6

You've finished drawing Einstein! Now you're a genius, too!

MARIE CURIE

LET'S DRAW THE FIRST WOMAN IN HISTORY TO WIN A NOBEL PRIZE! MARIE CURIE WAS A POLISH-FRENCH SCIENTIST AND A PHYSICIST WHO DISCOVERED RADIATION, LEADING TO BREAKTHROUGHS IN THE TREATMENT OF CANCER AND MANY OTHER SCIENTIFIC ADVANCES.

First, draw the guidelines to form her body.

0

1

2

Next, draw Marie's face shape and ear.

3

Then, draw her eyes and other facial features.

4

Draw her hair and bun.

Start sketching her upper body and hands.

5

Next, draw the test tubes she is holding and then her dress.

6

Once you're finished, she should look like this. Show off your drawing experiment!

THOMAS EDISON

HERE'S A CHANCE TO DRAW AMERICA'S GREATEST INVENTOR, THOMAS EDISON! HE INVENTED THE PHONOGRAPH, THE MOTION PICTURE CAMERA AND THE ELECTRIC LIGHT BULB, ALL OF WHICH HAVE MADE SO MUCH POSSIBLE IN THE MODERN WORLD.

Let's begin sketching the body guidelines.

1

Now draw his face shape and his hair.

2

Time to add Thomas's facial features.

3

Then, draw his bowtie and collar of his shirt.

4

5

Move on to adding his arms and upper body.

Add his legs in a sitting position.

6

Go ahead and add his shoes.

7

8

Lastly, draw the chair he is sitting on as well as the light bulb in his hand.

Brilliant! Once everything has been drawn, pat yourself on the back – you've just drawn Thomas Edison!

KATHERINE JOHNSON

MATHEMATICIAN KATHERINE JOHNSON WAS ONE OF THE FIRST AFRICAN-AMERICAN WOMEN TO WORK AS A NASA SCIENTIST. HER CALCULATIONS HELPED NASA LAUNCH THEIR FIRST MANNED SPACEFLIGHTS IN THE 1960s. IT'S YOUR MISSION TO DRAW HER!

Begin with drawing her basic guidelines.

1

Now draw her face shape as well as her hairline and hair.

2

Next, sketch in her facial features.

3

Then, draw the cat-eye glasses that frame her eyes.

4

Now add her upper body, shirt collar and NASA badge.

5

Finish the details of her upper body.

6

7

Now draw her skirt and high heels.

Give yourself a big thumbs up, you've figured out how to draw Katherine Johnson! Now add some colour!

ADA LOVELACE

THOUGHT TO HAVE BEEN THE FIRST COMPUTER PROGRAMMER, ADA LOVELACE WAS BORN IN 1815, THE DAUGHTER OF LORD BYRON, AND WAS A MATHEMATICIAN WITH A BRILLIANT ANALYTICAL MIND – LET'S WORK OUT HOW TO DRAW HER IN SEVEN STEPS!

Begin with the simple guidelines for Ada's head and body.

1

Then, draw the head shape as well as her two hair buns.

2

Now fill in her facial features.

3

Next, draw her floral hairpiece.

4

Then draw her scarf-like collar.

5

Sketch in her arm and then her dress.

6

Lastly, draw the flowery pattern on her dress.

7

All finished! If you feel like something is missing from the equation, add some more colour to Ada's outfit.

Ada Lovelace • **47**

NIKOLA TESLA

SERBIAN-AMERICAN INVENTOR NIKOLA TESLA IS BEST KNOWN FOR HIS DESIGN OF THE MODERN ALTERNATING CURRENT (AC) ELECTRICITY SUPPLY SYSTEM. FOR A BIT OF FUN ADD A POWERFUL ELECTRICAL CURRENT ABOVE HIM, AS EVERYONE THOUGHT HE WAS A MAGICIAN IN HIS DAY!

Start with the guidelines for Nikola.

Then, draw his face shape, ears and his hair.

Next, draw his facial features; don't forget to draw his moustache!

Sketch his upper body and hands. Start with his tie first.

Then, draw his legs and shoes.

Lastly, draw the electrical current above him.

What colour is electricity? Add your own choice to the glowing current above Nikola!

STEVE JOBS

THE CO-FOUNDER AND FORMER CEO OF APPLE, STEVE JOBS WAS THE VISIONARY COMPUTER SCIENTIST RESPONSIBLE FOR THE iPHONE, iPOD AND iPAD. HE WAS ALSO FAMOUS FOR HIS BASIC UNIFORM OF A BLACK POLO NECK, BLUE JEANS AND TRAINERS, ALL OF WHICH WE'LL INCLUDE HERE – LET'S GET STARTED!

Begin with the simple guides to shape Steve's body.

1

Then, draw a circle shape for his head.

2

3

Next, draw his hairline and ears.

Now draw his facial features and glasses.

4

Sketch his upper body and a phone in his hand.

5

6

Then, finish off by drawing his legs and shoes. Don't forget his other hand!

Here's the finished drawing, ready to be coloured in. Good job!

ISAAC NEWTON

GET YOUR PENCILS READY FOR ISAAC NEWTON! BORN IN 1642, HE WAS A MATHEMATICIAN, PHYSICIST AND ASTRONOMER. HIS THEORY OF GRAVITY CHANGED THE WORLD — HE OFTEN SAID HE WAS INSPIRED TO FORMULATE HIS THEORY WHILE WATCHING AN APPLE FALL FROM A TREE.

Start with the simple guides for Isaac.

1

Next, sketch the shape of his face and hairline.

2

Then, draw his big curls of hair.

3

Now fill in his facial features.

Then, start sketching the upper torso and an apple in his hand.

Next, sketch his robe.

Finish by drawing the rest of the robe's details.

What colour is the apple? Add some more details to bring Isaac to life!

SACAGAWEA

TIME TO DRAW SACAGAWEA, THE SHOSHONE WOMAN WHO TRAVELED THOUSANDS OF MILES WITH THE LEWIS AND CLARK EXPEDITION, FROM NORTH DAKOTA TO THE PACIFIC OCEAN. SHE HELPED THE EXPLORERS ESTABLISH CONTACT WITH DIFFERENT NATIVE AMERICAN POPULATIONS THROUGHOUT NORTH AMERICA. HER KNOWLEDGE OF THE NATURAL WORLD MADE HER ESSENTIAL TO THEIR TEAM.

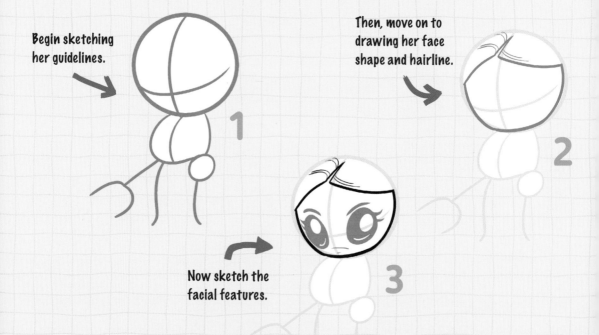

Begin sketching her guidelines.

1

Then, move on to drawing her face shape and hairline.

2

Now sketch the facial features.

3

4

After, draw her hair in two pigtails.

Next, draw her ear and then her upper body.

5

Start sketching her dress and its details.

6

7

After, draw her moccasins. Take your time.

Lastly, finish by drawing her staff.

8

Now that you've completed drawing Sacagawea, turn the page for your next adventure in drawing!

AMELIA EARHART

IN 1932, AMELIA EARHART BECAME THE FIRST FEMALE PILOT TO FLY SOLO ACROSS THE ATLANTIC OCEAN, BECOMING A WORLDWIDE CELEBRITY AND INSPIRATION FOR OTHER ADVENTUROUS YOUNG PEOPLE. HER DISAPPEARANCE IN 1937, WHILE ATTEMPTING TO FLY AROUND THE GLOBE, CONTINUES TO REMAIN A MYSTERY. LET'S DRAW THIS FEARLESS PIONEER!

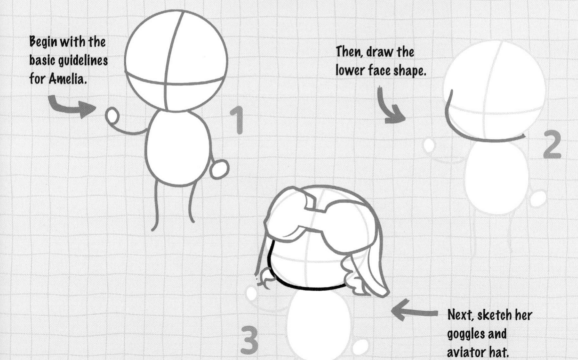

Begin with the basic guidelines for Amelia.

1

Then, draw the lower face shape.

2

3

Next, sketch her goggles and aviator hat.

Now draw her facial features.

Then, draw the interiors of the goggles.

4

5

6

Let's work on her upper body and hands.

7

Lastly, sketch the lower body.

Add some colour to your finished drawing, and you're ready for takeoff!

MAE JEMISON

GET YOUR PAPER AND PENCILS READY AND START THE COUNTDOWN TO DRAW MAE JEMISON, THE FIRST AFRICAN-AMERICAN WOMAN TO TRAVEL INTO SPACE! A FORMER ASTRONAUT FOR NASA, SHE WAS A MISSION SPECIALIST ON BOARD THE SPACE SHUTTLE 'ENDEAVOUR' IN 1992.

Begin by sketching the guides that will frame Mae's body and head.

1

Next, sketch her face, starting with the head shape.

2

Now draw her eyes and eyebrows.

3

Draw the ring for her space suit below her head.

Next, draw her upper body and hands holding her helmet.

Lastly, shade in the reflection on her helmet, then add her legs and the emblems on her space suit.

Phew, that was hard work, but look what you've accomplished! Impressive!

NEIL ARMSTRONG

SPACE FANS WILL LOVE THIS TUTORIAL OF NEIL ARMSTRONG, AN AMERICAN ASTRONAUT AND THE FIRST PERSON TO WALK ON THE MOON – MAKING HISTORY IN 1969. AS HE TOOK HIS FIRST STEPS, HE FAMOUSLY SAID: 'THAT'S ONE SMALL STEP FOR [A] MAN, ONE GIANT LEAP FOR MANKIND'.

Let's draw the basic guidelines for Neil.

1

Then, sketch in his face shape and hairline, as well as his ear.

2

Next, draw the rest of his hair and details.

3

Now draw the facial features for Neil.

4

Sketch his torso, beginning with the arms.

5

Then, draw his neck and legs.

6

7

Now work on the rest of the space suit and his helmet!

When you're finished drawing, add some colour to the flag and NASA badge. Great job!

DAVID BOWIE

AUDREY HEPBURN

BEYONCE

BRUCE LEE

SELENA

OPRAH WINFREY

CARMEN MIRANDA

MARILYN MONROE

ELVIS PRESLEY

ENTERTAINERS

MISTY COPELAND

DAVID BOWIE

VISIONARY, COLOURFUL AND FLAMBOYANT, DAVID BOWIE TRANSFORMED POP MUSIC IN THE '70s AND '80s. HERE'S A CHANCE TO DRAW ONE OF HIS MOST ICONIC LOOKS WITH A LIGHTNING BOLT PAINTED ACROSS HIS FACE, USED ON THE COVER OF HIS ALBUM ALADDIN SANE.

Begin by drawing the basic guides.

1

Then, draw Bowie's face shape and hairline.

2

Next, let's complete his hair.

3

Draw in the facial features for Bowie.

4

Then, add the lightning bolt across his face.

5

Draw the lapels of his top – make them wide!

6

Draw his legs and torso.

7

Then, draw his arms, hands and boots.

8

Get Bowie ready for the stage by adding some brilliant colour!

AUDREY HEPBURN

BELGIAN-BORN ACTOR, PHILANTHROPIST AND FASHION ICON AUDREY HEPBURN IS CONSIDERED TO BE ONE OF THE MOST STYLISH AND ELEGANT SCREEN STARS IN CINEMATIC HISTORY. THE LOOK WE'RE GOING TO DRAW HERE IS INSPIRED BY HER MOST FAMOUS FILM ROLE – HOLLY GOLIGHTLY IN *BREAKFAST AT TIFFANY'S*.

Begin by drawing her body guidelines.

1

Then, draw her face shape and ear with an earring, as well as her fringe.

2

Next, draw her bun and back of her hairline.

3

4

Next, draw Audrey's facial features.

5

Now draw her body, from top to bottom, don't forget to add a pearl necklace.

6

Then, finish by drawing a belt, the rest of her arm and glove details.

She's ready for the red carpet! Shade her dress with elegant black.

BEYONCÉ

HAVING SOLD MORE THAN ONE HUNDRED MILLION ALBUMS, BEYONCÉ IS ONE OF THE MOST FAMOUS SINGERS AND DANCERS IN THE WORLD, WHO HAS INFLUENCED A GENERATION OF YOUNG BLACK WOMEN. LET'S DRAW THE MULTI-TALENTED QUEEN B!

Draw the simple guide shapes.

1

Then, draw Bey's face shape.

2

Next, let's draw her facial features.

3

Now add a big bun with long hair below it.

Time to draw her body! Begin with her torso first.

4

5

Finish the body and then add Beyoncé's outfit and boots!

6

What a workout! Now add some colour and sparkle to this amazing performer.

BRUCE LEE

NOW LET'S DRAW BRUCE LEE, ONE OF THE MOST ICONIC MARTIAL ARTISTS OF ALL TIME. WITH HIS POPULARITY AND INFLUENCE AS AN ACTOR AND DIRECTOR, HE HELPED TO CHANGE THE WAY ASIAN PEOPLE ARE REPRESENTED ON SCREEN. LET'S PAY TRIBUTE TO BRUCE LEE'S REMARKABLE CAREER WITH A DRAWING!

Build the guidelines for Bruce by sketching basic shapes for his body.

1

Then, add the hair shape to frame his head.

2

Next, draw his face and hairline.

3

Now sketch in his facial features.

4

5

Next, draw his fists and arms, ready for action!

6

Sketch in more of his upper and lower body.

7

Then, draw his belt and shoes.

Is your completed drawing ready to do kung fu?

SELENA

WIDELY FOLLOWED AND CELEBRATED IN THE 1990s, SELENA QUINTANILLA-PÉREZ WAS AN INSPIRATIONAL MEXICAN-AMERICAN SINGER WHO WAS NAMED 'QUEEN OF TEJANO MUSIC'. SHE WAS ALSO FAMOUS FOR HER UNIQUE SENSE OF STYLE – LET'S TRY TO CAPTURE HER BOLD SPIRIT IN THIS DRAWING!

Begin by drawing the body guidelines for Selena.

1

Next, work on the face shape, earrings and her hair that frames her face.

2

Now draw the facial features.

3

Move on to her
hands and arms.

4

Next, draw her
clothing with
her coat on top.

5

Draw the rest of
her outfit and
body, making sure
you work your
way down to
her shoes.

6

Now that you've
drawn Selena,
add some colour
and detail to her
outfit. Amazing!

OPRAH WINFREY

HAVE YOUR PENS AT THE READY TO DRAW THIS FABULOUS SUPERSTAR! OPRAH WINFREY IS BEST KNOWN FOR HER POPULAR TELEVISION TALK SHOW, WHICH RAN FOR TWENTY-FIVE YEARS. OPRAH IS BELOVED FOR HER GENEROSITY AND CHARITABLE CONTRIBUTIONS. SHE IS ONE OF THE MOST ICONIC AFRICAN-AMERICAN WOMEN IN HISTORY, AND AMERICA'S FIRST BLACK MULTI-BILLIONAIRE.

Start with the basic guides to draw Oprah.

1

Then, draw her classic cat-eye glasses.

2

3

Now sketch her facial features and eyes behind the glasses.

4 Next, draw her face shape.

Then, sketch her curly hair and earrings.

5

6 Sketch in her upper body and dress.

7 Lastly, draw her feet and legs.

Choose some vibrant, fun colours and colour in your drawing!

CARMEN MIRANDA

NICKNAMED THE 'BRAZILIAN BOMBSHELL' BACK IN THE 1940s, THERE ARE LOTS OF ACCESSORIES TO ADD TO FILM AND FASHION ICON CARMEN MIRANDA! SHE WAS FAMOUS FOR HER SINGING, DANCING AND UNFORGETTABLE FRUIT HAT. LET'S RECREATE THIS SAMBA PERFORMER – AND HER FAMOUS HAT!

Begin with the basic guidelines for her figure.

1

Draw her face shape, hairline and ears with big hoop earrings.

2

Next, draw her facial features!

3

4

Then, draw her famous fruit hat, with a little bit of hair showing underneath.

5

Next, sketch her upper body and her maracas.

6

Now sketch Carmen's dress and bottom ruffles.

7

Then, draw her legs and dress details.

There's plenty to colour in once you've finished Carmen's spectacular outfit!

MARILYN MONROE

HOLLYWOOD'S SWEETHEART, INSTANTLY RECOGNIZABLE WITH HER PLATINUM BLONDE HAIR AND RED LIPSTICK, MARILYN MONROE WAS A TALENTED ACTOR AND FASHION ICON. LET'S CELEBRATE HER IN THIS DRAWING INSPIRED BY A FAMOUS SCENE FROM *THE SEVEN YEAR ITCH*.

Start with the basic guidelines for Marilyn.

1

Then, draw the face shape and outline her hairline.

2

Next, draw her iconic hairstyle.

3

4

Now draw her facial features!

5

Then, draw her upper body and hands.

6

Sketch in the dress that she is trying to push down.

7

Finish by sketching her legs and shoes.

Is your drawing ready for the walk of fame?

ELVIS PRESLEY

THE BEST SELLING SOLO ARTIST IN THE HISTORY OF RECORDED MUSIC, ROCK 'N' ROLL MUSICIAN AND ACTOR ELVIS BECAME A GLOBAL ICON IN THE '50s AND '60s – EVENTUALLY HE WAS NICKNAMED SIMPLY 'THE KING'. LET'S DRAW THIS LEGEND!

Begin by drawing the essential guidelines for Elvis.

1

Then, draw the King's face shape, as well as his hairline.

2

Next, draw his pompadour and sideburns.

3

Now let's sketch his facial features.

Next, draw his upper body, arm and hand.

5

Now sketch his lower body and trousers.

6

7

Lastly, finish the rest of his clothing and then add the microphone he is holding.

Your Elvis is ready for some 'Jailhouse Rock'! Now add some colour.

MISTY COPELAND

GET YOUR PENCILS READY TO DRAW AMERICAN BALLET DANCER MISTY COPELAND. SHE IS THE FIRST AFRICAN-AMERICAN PRINCIPAL DANCER IN THE 75-YEAR HISTORY OF THE AMERICAN BALLET THEATRE. HER PERFORMANCES ARE EXTRAORDINARY TO WATCH AS SHE GRACEFULLY TAKES HOLD OF THE STAGE.

Start with the simple guidelines to shape her body and pose.

1

2

Then, sketch her face shape and hair.

3

Sketch her eyes and mouth.

Let's start on her pose! Work down from her torso to her pointe shoes.

4

Fill in her arms and then start on her leotard. Finish Misty's hair.

5

6

Now add the rest of her beautiful flowing dress!

Once you're done, you should have something very similar to this. Bravo!

FRIDA KAHLO

PABLO PICASSO

MARY SHELLEY

MAYA ANGELOU

WILLIAM SHAKESPEARE

J.K. ROWLING

VINCENT VAN GOGH

ANNA WINTOUR

ANDY WARHOL

LEONARDO DA VINCI

ANNE FRANK

ARTISTS AND WRITERS

EDGAR ALLAN POE

FRIDA KAHLO

TIME TO DRAW FRIDA KAHLO, ONE OF THE MOST FAMOUS ARTISTS OF THE TWENTIETH CENTURY. HER COLOURFUL SELF-PORTRAITS, FEATURING FLOWERS, ANIMALS AND FRUIT, WERE INSPIRED BY THE FOLK ART AND NATURAL SETTINGS OF HER NATIVE MEXICO.

Draw the basic guides for Frida's head and body.

1

Draw her face and simple hair shape.

2

Add her distinctive eyebrows, then her eyes, followed by the rest of her face.

3

Next, draw ears and hoop earrings to frame her face.

4

Draw the collar around her neck.

Then, draw her left shoulder and left arm.

Add her right shoulder and right arm.

Next, draw the skirt of her dress.

Lastly, draw the flowers in the centre of her head.

After everything is drawn to your liking, you can start colouring her in!

PABLO PICASSO

LET'S LEARN TO DRAW ONE OF THE MOST CREATIVE ARTISTS IN HISTORY! PICASSO WAS A PROLIFIC SPANISH PAINTER AND SCULPTOR WHO CO-FOUNDED THE ABSTRACT STYLE OF CUBISM AND INFLUENCED THE DEVELOPMENT OF MODERN ART. HIS PAINTINGS HAVE SOLD FOR HUNDREDS OF MILLIONS OF POUNDS.

Start off by drawing the simple guidelines.

1

Then, draw Picasso's head shape.

2

3

Now draw the hair framing his face and the ear.

Next, draw Picasso's facial features – make sure you add wrinkles!

4

Now draw his arms raised, holding a paintbrush.

5

Draw the rest of his body and shoes.

6

7

Finish by drawing the iconic stripes on his t-shirt and finish the details of his trousers.

Step back and admire your masterpiece!

MARY SHELLEY

ARE YOU READY TO DRAW NOVELIST MARY SHELLEY, AUTHOR OF *FRANKENSTEIN?* MARY WAS ONLY EIGHTEEN WHEN SHE STARTED THE STORY – THOUGHT TO BE THE FIRST WORK OF SCIENCE FICTION – ABOUT A SCIENTIST AND HIS FRIGHTENING CREATION. SHELLEY'S NOVEL CONTINUES TO BE HUGELY INFLUENTIAL IN POP CULTURE.

Draw Mary's head and body guidelines first.

1

Next, draw the head shape.

2

Move on to draw the hair that frames her head.

3

Now draw her eyes and mouth.

4

Let's start working on her upper body and draw the arms.

5

6

Using thin lines, draw her collar and waist.

7

Lastly, finish the rest of her dress.

Look what you created! Fantastic!

MAYA ANGELOU

AFRICAN-AMERICAN WRITER, POET AND ACTOR MAYA ANGELOU'S MOST FAMOUS WORK IS HER MEMOIR *I KNOW WHY THE CAGED BIRD SINGS*. SHE WAS ALSO A CIVIL RIGHTS ACTIVIST WHO WORKED WITH MARTIN LUTHER KING JR. LET'S HONOUR HER LEGACY WITH A DRAWING!

Draw the simple guidelines for the head and body.

1

Sketch Maya's head first, and then her facial features.

2

Now shade the insides of her eyes.

3

Work on
drawing her
head wrap next.

Sketch the torso,
starting with
her collar and
then the arms.

4

5

Draw her hands
and the dress.

6

7

Don't forget to
draw her shoes!

Add colour and
pattern to Maya's
outfit when
your drawing
is finished.

WILLIAM SHAKESPEARE

LET'S PUT PEN TO PAPER AND DRAW THE WORLD'S MOST FAMOUS PLAYWRIGHT, WILLIAM SHAKESPEARE! HIS PLAYS — WHICH INCLUDE ROMEO AND JULIET, MACBETH, A MIDSUMMER NIGHT'S DREAM AND MANY OTHERS — ARE PERFORMED MORE OFTEN THAN THOSE OF ANY OTHER DRAMATIST.

First, draw the basic guidelines for his body.

1

Then, draw William's facial features, plus moustache and goatee.

2

Next, begin drawing his face shape and ear.

3

Now draw his wavy hair and earring.

4

Then, add his body, beginning with the ruff around his neck.

5

6

Next, draw the legs and vest.

Finish off by drawing his beard, the quill pen and trouser seam!

7

Your finished drawing should look like this. Applause!

J.K. ROWLING

LET'S CONJURE A GREAT DRAWING OF BRITISH AUTHOR J.K. ROWLING, WHO WROTE THE HARRY POTTER NOVELS, THE HIGHEST SELLING BOOK SERIES IN HISTORY. SHE HAS MADE A HUGE IMPACT ON THE WORLD WITH HER MAGICAL WORLD AND BELOVED CHARACTERS.

Begin by drawing the basic guidelines for her body and head.

1

Next, sketch her face shape as well as her hair to frame her forehead. Add earrings to her ears.

2

Then, draw her facial features.

3

Complete her head by finishing her hair.

4

Work on her body next, starting with her arms.

5

6

Then, add her necklaces and collar.

7

Next, draw her book!

8

Finish by drawing her legs and shoes!

Once you're all done, your drawing will look like this. Magic!

VINCENT VAN GOGH

LET'S PAY TRIBUTE TO THE AMAZING TALENT OF POST-IMPRESSIONIST PAINTER, VINCENT VAN GOGH, ONE OF THE MOST VISIONARY ARTISTS IN HISTORY. HE WAS FAMOUS FOR HIS EXPRESSIVE BRUSHSTROKES AND VIBRANT USE OF COLOUR. VAN GOGH CREATED OVER 2,000 WORKS OF ART IN HIS LIFETIME.

First, draw the body guidelines for Vincent's pose.

1

Now draw the lower part of his face, his beard and ear.

2

Next, add the hair to frame his face and head shape.

3

Then draw his facial features.

4

Sketch in the upper body, with one hand holding a paintbrush and the other holding a canvas.

5

Finish by drawing his legs and shoes.

6

Take a bow – you've just drawn Vincent van Gogh!

ANNA WINTOUR

THE ONE AND ONLY ANNA WINTOUR HAS BEEN THE EDITOR-IN-CHIEF OF AMERICAN VOGUE SINCE 1988. HER ORIGINAL STYLE AND GENEROUS SUPPORT FOR YOUNG DESIGNERS HAS INFLUENCED THE FASHION INDUSTRY AROUND THE WORLD.

Draw guidelines for Anna's head and body.

1

Let's start with her fringe and her iconic bob hairstyle.

2

Now add her chin, mouth and sunglasses.

3

Then, draw her necklace and fluffy wrap.

4

Lastly, draw her dress and the pattern details.

5

When finished, your drawing will be front-cover ready!

ANDY WARHOL

IN THIS TUTORIAL YOU'RE GOING TO DRAW ANDY WARHOL, AN ICONIC POP ARTIST WHO DEFINED THE 1960s. WARHOL'S MOST FAMOUS WORKS ARE SCREENPRINTS OF CAMPBELL'S SOUP CANS AND CELEBRITIES LIKE MARILYN MONROE.

Let's start by drawing the face and body guides for Andy.

1

Next, draw his face shape and eyes.

2

Then, draw his glasses, mouth and eyebrows.

3

Now draw his iconic platinum hair.

Next, draw the torso and hands holding his camera.

4

5

Lastly, sketch his lower body and shoes.

6

Your end result should look like this. Great practice!

LEONARDO DA VINCI

GET YOUR PENCILS READY TO DRAW ONE OF THE MOST LEGENDARY PAINTERS AND INVENTORS OF THE ITALIAN RENAISSANCE, LEONARDO DA VINCI. HIS MOST FAMOUS PAINTING IS THE 'MONA LISA', WHICH HANGS IN THE LOUVRE MUSEUM IN PARIS, FRANCE, AND IS SEEN BY ABOUT 30,000 VISITORS EACH DAY.

Start with the simple guidelines for Leonardo.

1

Next, draw his hat and hair that frame his face.

2

3

Now draw his long beard.

4 Complete his head by drawing his facial features.

5 Draw the right side of his body, with his hand holding the paint palette.

Then, draw the left side of his body, adding a paintbrush in his hand.

6

7 Finish by drawing his lower body.

Voilà! Now you're a legend.

ANNE FRANK

ANNE FRANK WAS ONLY THIRTEEN YEARS OLD WHEN SHE AND HER FAMILY HAD TO GO INTO HIDING FROM THE NAZIS DURING WORLD WAR II. HER FAMOUS DIARY OF HER EXPERIENCE OF BEING A JEWISH PERSON DURING THAT TIME HAS AFFECTED MILLIONS OF PEOPLE AROUND THE GLOBE. LET'S DRAW THIS BRAVE HEROINE.

Begin by drawing the guides for Anne's pose.

1

Then, draw her hair and face shape.

2

Keep working on her hair so that it frames her face shape!

3

5

Now sketch the collar of her shirt and her pendants.

Next, work on her facial features.

4

Then, draw her dress, legs and shoes.

6

Lastly, draw the journal and pen in her hands.

7

This is what your finished drawing should look like. Well done!

EDGAR ALLAN POE

NINETEENTH-CENTURY AMERICAN WRITER EDGAR ALLAN POE WAS FAMOUS FOR HIS DARK AND MYSTERIOUS POEMS AND SHORT STORIES. WE WILL BE DRAWING HIM WITH A RAVEN FRIEND, 'NEVERMORE', INSPIRED BY HIS MOST FAMOUS POEM, *THE RAVEN*.

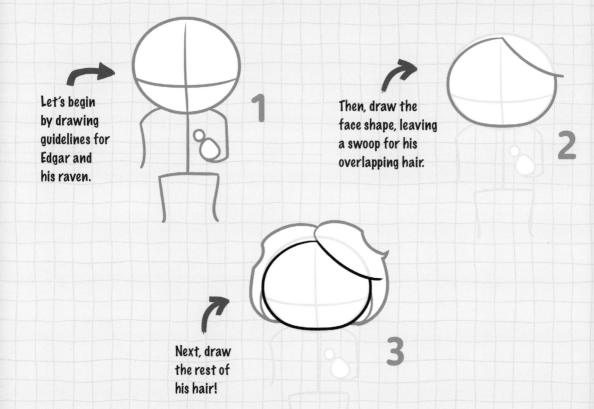

Let's begin by drawing guidelines for Edgar and his raven.

1

Then, draw the face shape, leaving a swoop for his overlapping hair.

2

Next, draw the rest of his hair!

3

Now draw his facial features and moustache.

4

Once that's done, sketch his upper body and raven.

5

6

Then, draw his suit and lower body.

7

Finish by drawing his trouser creases and shoes.

This is what you should finish with. Excellent work!

MUHAMMAD ALI

SERENA WILLIAMS

USAIN BOLT

SIMONE BILES

MEGAN RAPINOE

MICHAEL JORDAN

BABE RUTH

MICHELLE KWAN

SPORTS FIGURES

MUHAMMAD ALI

'FLOAT LIKE A BUTTERFLY, STING LIKE A BEE', IS A FAMOUS QUOTE FROM OLYMPIC GOLD MEDALLIST, MUHAMMAD ALI. HE CALLED HIMSELF 'THE GREATEST' AFTER WINNING DOZENS OF HEAVYWEIGHT CHAMPIONSHIPS – ALI IS ONE OF THE MOST CELEBRATED ATHLETES OF ALL TIME.

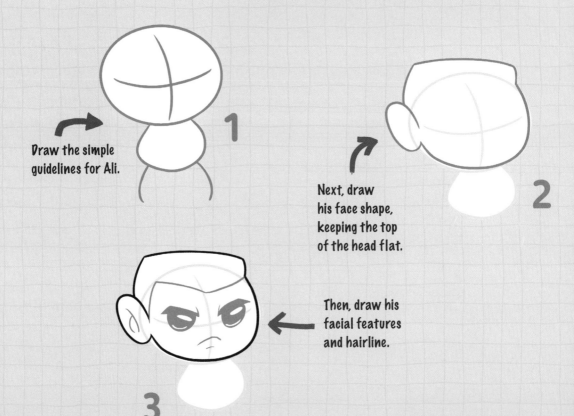

Draw the simple guidelines for Ali.

1

Next, draw his face shape, keeping the top of the head flat.

2

Then, draw his facial features and hairline.

3

Fill in his hair with black, leaving a thin line for the highlight.

4

Draw boxing gloves on each side of his body.

5

Now sketch his shorts.

6

7

Finish drawing him by adding his legs and shoes!

For the next round you can add colour and shadows to your heavyweight champion!

SERENA WILLIAMS

TENNIS SUPERSTAR SERENA WILLIAMS (FORMERLY NO. 1 IN THE WORLD) HAS WON MORE MAJOR SINGLES TITLES THAN ANY MAN OR WOMAN IN THE LAST SIXTY YEARS. ARE YOU READY TO DRAW THIS TRAILBLAZING ATHLETE WHO HAS INSPIRED A WHOLE NEW GENERATION OF TENNIS PLAYERS?

Begin by drawing the basic guidelines for Serena.

1

Then, draw her head shape and headband.

2

Next, draw her hair and hairline.

3

4

Now, draw her facial features as well.

5

Next, sketch her arm and hands that will be holding the tennis racket.

Then, draw her racket.

6

Let's add the strings to her racket and draw the grip as well.

7

8

Lastly, draw the tennis ball and her lower body.

Congrats! You've finished drawing Serena!

USAIN BOLT

HOLDER OF WORLD RECORDS FOR THE 100M, 200M AND THE 4 X 100M RELAY, JAMAICAN ATHLETE USAIN BOLT IS CONSIDERED TO BE THE GREATEST SPRINTER OF ALL TIME AND THE FASTEST MAN ALIVE. HE IS WELL-KNOWN FOR HIS FAMOUS STANCE – LET'S DRAW THIS LEGEND!

Begin by drawing the guidelines for Usain.

1

2

Now sketch his head shape.

3

Next, draw his hairline, eyes, ear and mouth.

Then, draw his raised arms in the 'lightning bolt' pose!

4

Don't forget to draw the lightning bolts on his t-shirt!

Let's draw his outfit and lower body.

5

6

Your finished drawing should look like this. Nice work crossing the finish line!

SIMONE BILES

SOAR TO NEW HEIGHTS BY CAPTURING THE POWER AND GRACE OF ONE OF THE TOP GYMNASTS IN THE WORLD, SIMONE BILES. SHE IS THE MOST DECORATED AMERICAN GYMNAST IN HISTORY, WITH THIRTY OLYMPIC AND WORLD CHAMPIONSHIP MEDALS AND COUNTING!

Begin by drawing Simone's body guidelines – you can already see her dynamic pose.

1

Move on to drawing her face shape, as well as her ponytail flowing upwards.

2

3

Next, draw her facial features and shade in the dark tone of her hair.

Now draw her
upper body with
outstretched
arms and chest.

Then, sketch her
lower body
performing a
midair split.

Lastly, add the medal
around her neck!

Once you've
completed all the
steps, show off the
finished drawing!
It looks awesome!

MEGAN RAPINOE

MEGAN RAPINOE PLAYS FOR THE US NATIONAL WOMEN'S SOCCER LEAGUE AND CO-CAPTAINS THE UNITED STATES NATIONAL TEAM. HER DEDICATION AND POSITIVE LEADERSHIP HELPED HER TEAM WIN THE WORLD CUP IN 2019. SHE IS ALSO AN OUTSPOKEN ADVOCATE FOR EQUAL PAY FOR WOMEN AND MANY LGBT+ CAUSES.

Lightly draw the guidelines for Megan's body and head.

1

Draw Megan's face shape first and then her facial features.

2

Then, draw her swept-back hair.

3

Then, draw the rest of her t-shirt and lower body.

4

Sketch her left arm and collar.

5

6

Fill in her right arm as well as her team emblems.

7

Finish by drawing a circle for the ball and filling in the pattern.

You've got skills – keep practicing!

MICHAEL JORDAN

LET'S JUMP TO IT AND DRAW MJ, THE ALL-TIME GREATEST PROFESSIONAL BASKETBALL PLAYER. NICKNAMED 'AIR JORDAN' FOR HIS FINESSE, HE PLAYED FIFTEEN SEASONS IN THE US NATIONAL BASKETBALL ASSOCIATION, WINNING SIX CHAMPIONSHIPS WITH HIS TEAM THE CHICAGO BULLS.

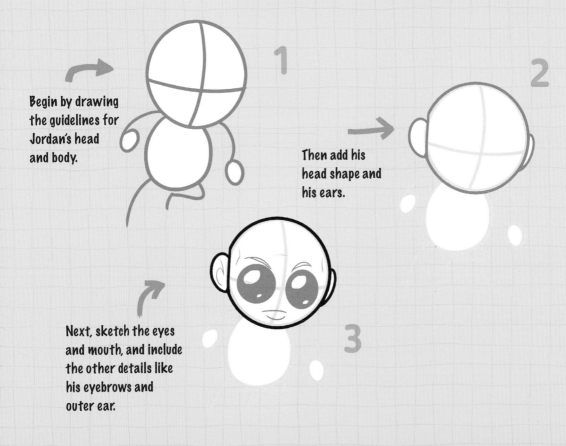

Begin by drawing the guidelines for Jordan's head and body.

1

Then add his head shape and his ears.

2

Next, sketch the eyes and mouth, and include the other details like his eyebrows and outer ear.

3

Then, draw his arms.

4

Draw his torso next.

5

Now add a basketball underneath his hand.

6

7

Draw the lower body and shorts.

8

Lastly, fill in his legs and shoes.

What a slam dunk! Now you can add some team colours!

BABE RUTH

LEGENDARY BASEBALL SUPERSTAR BABE RUTH PLAYED IN TWENTY-TWO US MAJOR LEAGUE BASEBALL SEASONS, FIRST FOR THE BOSTON RED SOX, THEN THE NEW YORK YANKEES. HE SET A NUMBER OF BASEBALL RECORDS – SOME OF WHICH STILL HAVEN'T BEEN BEATEN. LET'S DRAW 'THE GREAT BAMBINO'!

Start by sketching the body guidelines for Babe Ruth.

1

2

Then, draw his face shape and ear.

Next, draw his baseball hat.

3

Now sketch in his facial features and ear detailing.

4

Then add his upper body as well.

5

6

Now sketch the lower body, adding his belt.

7

Lastly, draw the baseball, bat, stripes on his uniform and his shoes.

You knocked it out of the park – time to share your drawing with admiring baseball fans. Home run!

MICHELLE KWAN

LET'S CELEBRATE THE REMARKABLE GRACE AND TALENT OF FIGURE SKATER MICHELLE KWAN. WITH DETERMINATION AND GRIT, SHE WON TWO OLYMPIC MEDALS AND MORE THAN FORTY US AND WORLD CHAMPIONSHIPS.

Start with the guides to shape Michelle's body.

1

Then, draw her face shape.

2

Now frame her face with her hair in a bun.

3

Now sketch her facial features.

Next, draw the top part of her costume.

4

5

Now draw her legs! Start from the waist and work down to the ice skates.

6

7

Lastly, draw her outstretched arms!

Wow, you've successfully drawn Michelle Kwan. Stay focused and continue practicing!